Milkweed Smithereens

Bernadette Mayer

Milkweed Smithereens

A NEW DIRECTIONS PAPERBOOK ORIGINAL

AUTHOR'S ACKNOWLEDGMENTS: This book includes a mixture of recent work and uncollected poems from the 1970s through the 1990s found in my archives at the University of California, San Diego. Thank you to Julie Levitan and Marie Warsh for their work collecting and organizing these poems. Some of the more recent poems have made previous appearances: "Pi-Day" and "On the Wild Strawberry" in the *Café Review*, "Lobelias of Fear" on poets.org, and "The Joys of Dahlias" in *Hurricane Review*. Thank you to Barbara for all her work on this book and for all the oysters.

Manufactured in the United States of America
First published as New Directions Paperbook 1546 in 2022

Library of Congress Cataloging-in-Publication Data
Names: Mayer, Bernadette, author.
Title: Milkweed smithereens / Bernadette Mayer.
Description: First edition. | New York : New Directions Books, 2022. |
Series: New Directions Paperbook ; 1546 | "A New Directions Paperbook original."
Identifiers: LCCN 2022037444 | ISBN 9780811229227 (paperback) |
ISBN 9780811229234 (ebook)
Subjects: LCGFT: Poetry.
Classification: LCC PS3563.A952 M56 2022 | DDC 811/.54—dc23/eng/20220808
LC record available at https://lccn.loc.gov/2022037444

10 9 8 7 6 5 4 3 2

New Directions Books are published for James Laughlin
by New Directions Publishing Corporation
80 Eighth Avenue, New York 10011

Milkweed Smithereens

Milkweed Smithereens

Asclepias
herbaceous plants with a milky juice
showy flowers
more or less poisonous
Asclepias syriaca a plant misnamed
dull red flowers very fragrant
young shoots eaten as asparagus
silklike down of the seeds employed
to stuff pillows
fiber woven into muslins,
made into paper
(from *Asclepias acida*
an intoxicating milky juice is squeezed
the home of the plant was in heaven
under its influence Indra
fixed the earth & sky in their place,
the Soma plant
removes death)
a common roadside weed (*syriaca*)
called "silkweed"
from the silky down which surmounts the seed
used for making hats
a long fine thread of a glossy whiteness
the anodyne properties of its root
in cases of asthma
and typhus attended with catarrh
the milky juice a domestic application
to warts
it contains Ascelpione
& caoutchouc, gum, sugar, salts
Asclepias incarnata
swamp milkweed
flowers rose-purple, fragrant,

disposed in terminal-crowded umbels
two to six on a peduncle 2 inches long
consisting of ten to twenty small flowers
two acrid resins
a dose of the powder
the *syriaca* in waste areas, roadsides, rich composted soils
collect the shoots when six inches high
most tender in the early morning
collect the pods when light green & soft
the flowers when in full bloom
beware of the bees
the early pods,
alone or with the purple fragrant flowers
may be prepared as fritters
or included in soups or stews
the stems in cream sauce
may be topped with buttered crumbs
a riot of milkweed close to the wigwam
neat soups thickened with buds & flowers
do become mucilaginous like okra when cooked
eaten before a feast so that a man
or woman could consume more food
the root for maladies
Linnaeus dedicated it to Aesculapius
of whose name Asclepias is a corruption
this Cinderella weed
has produced food
not only in its shoots & pods but in the seeds
the meal residue is now used
for stock feed
the stalk & silk (floss) of the pods
made featherweight clothing
the fleshy roots
when broken in pieces
form new plants
the shoots are washed well

& steamed until soft
like asparagus
one should gather quantities of
seeds of the more prolific growers
such as burdock dandelion milkweed & evening primrose
plant the seeds in rich but not over composted soil
contained in flower-pots, indoor window boxes
or even in decorated tin cans
latex a milky liquid
in rubber trees, milkweed & poppy
the basis of rubber
plant from *planus* level flat (ground for sowing)
any living thing that cannot move voluntarily
has no sense organs & makes its own food
by photosynthesis
any tree shrub herb usually soft-stemmed
a young one, ready to put into other soil
for growth to maturity
a slip cutting or set

The Joys of Dahlias

ahoy matey, I'm peeling your lollipop
dear darling and all that jazz, are you the
bride to be or just the ladies' choice
or maybe the amber queen, an american beauty
or a squirrel posing in a birdbath
awe shucks, what a cute rabbit as dazzling
as an Azteca, I'd be yellowish-orange
like a word or a flamethrower, or dream catcher
that is fuchsia, baby red is baby yellow
I am so happy in my bed beep beep who did it?
blah blah blah it's blue satin bliss
the bishop of York wants some blackberry ice
the blue bayou is bluetiful, bonnie Esperance
is blue purple-urple or more like bridezilla?
John Lurie's brushstrokes bumble rumble
in my caliente cafe au lait, is it enchanted?
we have candlelight at center court for Brooklyn
cha ching, cheers for the cap cherry drops
but they're chewy, Mr. Cherubino Chickadee
and the cloudburst brother, Daniel and Jonas
I invited my coral gypsy over for cornish hens
and cupcakes on Tuesday but instead came
daddy's girl and the dancing queen, double trouble
but deputy Bob, also a firefighter, took care of it
e z duzzit we felt. Me and Einstein and Emory Paul
Elijah Mason and the flame throwing enchantress
we were told to call them Delilah's Fluffles
sleep now, smart pants or the midnight dancer
will tutti frutti your fabulous memory
        toodle-oo

Obsidian Butterflies

not too quickly
do they fly away
someday soon casually
when spring comes

from *The Covid Diary*

it's the wind I'm hearing next day, 2 stinkbugs, 1 fly, 1 sun that doesn't make
much warmth on the still-green field, can you feel sorry for a field? i feel
sorry for myself though i'm smarter than the field maybe, but not as smart as
nabokov, as we both go around criticizing everything, but poor nabokov didn't
understand about whales' memories of the future, how come?

a memory is nothing
nothing is a memory
    i wish i was something
    the size of a squirrel
    i'd not need a president then
    or worry what is democracy!

the quarantine began on phil's b'day, march 14, we were having a little party
in beacon so friends from here & friends from nyc could come. then marie said
she couldn't because she was in an office with the woman who was married
to the head of something large & he had the corona virus. so when kids say,
"you started it" we could say that to marie, but it was actually already started
somewhere else by someone else, like the kid who left a lobster at my doorstep,
freddie stegel did it! now it is june 10, cloudy & windy, a tree

Disruption of Distance

it's right there now
if you wanna see
& in the quantum world
there is no causation, things
might happen differently from
the way you thought, don't bother thinking
get on a deer, we could save the lions
but not the rhinoceros because of poaching

      dear fellow honky tonk angels
      please come over here right now
      change my envelopes from pink
      to goldenrod & then
      i saw you changed them back again
      what are you thinking?
      there are signs saying
      don't cut the trees down
      but you can fish here
      but don't cut the fish down
      you can make ribose
      but don't cut down on poems

you might fall on your head or lightning strike you in the middle of the field. is a peafowl a peacock?

what is the furthest thing? an adirondack chair? could be, the sun on the gold-enrod paper goes in squiggly lines, but why? there are as many questions as declarative sentences, you know, do you know? once you know, will you know forever? like a still picture of a stream flowing, river flowing, the ides of june, 2020, & what a mess it all is. trump's gotten rid of all environmental deterrents to climate change, hasn't used obama's ideas for combatting a pandemic & has created doubts about the chance of his leaving office if he loses the election, i can't think of a way it could be worse, rumor has it that people demonstrating about the death of george floyd will create a second wave of the virus, i just walk in the field, everything's overgrown, i can walk in the forest more easily following bill's tire tracks, i keep this journal & it seems like things only happen when phil's home. there's a blue jay at the birdbath which has water in it.

the stinkbugs seem to be staying more together, that is with each other, than before & flying like birds, the shadow of the bug is something to see, a couple of ladybugs too, i know who i'd root for in a bug war.

Shadow Biosphere

to make ribose
coat an interstellar dust grain
in water, methanol
& ammonia ices
bake under ultraviolet light
from a young star
if you succeed
it will breathe
every thousand years

it's friday june 26 at the beginning, middle or end of the pandemic, it's not any of those things—it's in the midst of the pandemic, i think the red-winged black-birds have taken over the western world, for humans the thing to do is stare.

early this morning, june 24, it poured & lightninged and the weather is cooler, less humid but wet, the bonsai tree died, i feel like a person drugged in a mental hospital staring into space. now the field is sunny.

rosemary & i used to push in my mother's breasts as play. she & my uncle have "ski" noses, "falsies" were used for the missing breast. swimming too my mother had a way of entering the water as if to do the breaststroke immediately. she said "you're leaving half the eggs in the pan" and "these carrots are earthy." she had a pressure cooker, shopped at bohack's, my father grew strawberries, candytufts, tea roses, bachelor buttons. He said my mother's favorite flower was a violet. there is something about all this that's shrouded in secrecy. how could they? how could it be? my mother read "anatomy of a murder" to distract herself, my father's favorite book was frankenstein, except that was probably a joke, so the point of writing it down is you can then forget all about it. so just this one last time, i beg you, whoever you are, let me forget all about it, i'm 75 years old, a lot of people are dying from this virus, i don't care if i do, but i'd like not to be so nervous all the time. the best story is when we got a 1954 chevrolet my mother passed the driving test easily but not my father, endless times he took it, also closed the trunk on his hand once. now the sun's behind a cloud, nope, back out again, brooklyn accents abounded—erl, the duke of earl, i liked ricky nelson, these are gloves from manhattan, the man who used to take me out in a taxi, shadows of leaves are on floors everywhere, teddy randazzo, knights of columbus, the spooky german beer halls where everybody played the harmonica, dancing the lindy with r, finding out how creepy he was.

Stephen Hawking

the distance
to alpha centauri
is so great, friends
that to reach it
in a human lifetime
a spacecraft would
have to carry roughly
fuel with the mass
of all the stars
in the galaxy

vladimir nabokov said:
> i confess i do not believe in time
> in BEING AND TIME, *poor heidegger*
> didn't finish the time part in time
> to publish it with the being part
> so everything-now must be not-being
> there is a pine needle stuck in the screen
> the side nearest me must be the being side
> the one further away's the time side
> nabokov only said the first line
> even when you have nothing to do
> there's not enough time in the day

there are 5 stinkbugs on the back porch—the stinkbugs don't make you feel good or likeable. but the one beautiful tree we have that i can see is still fulsome. in years past it's always been the best & most long-lasting foliage tree & now, even in this year of all the leaves blown down & drabness, as i see it, it's a glorious tree between the locusts, acting as if there's not a stinkbug around.

if i'm so smart how come i don't have another typewriter? i'd like to know what the word indexicality means too.

this will be a little test to see if expressive(?) writing is a cure for the malaise of the coronavirus. well it doesn't cure the pain in my left knee, there is something wrong with my stomach which is nerves. walking home from church, the daily news magazine had elvis presley who r & i were forbidden to listen to on the cover. when i got home i found out that my father had died, i was 12. the local parish priest was there, did he come on to me? do you want to see him (my father)? I said no. he'd died in the bathroom. he'd been home from work with muscle spasms, at least that's what i was told. then i got my period for the first time. my mother already had breast cancer & had lost a breast. my homelife was a nightmare, later my uncle took us out to buy us records. i felt that this was a very weird idea, replacing my father with an LP? i helped pick out what my father would wear in his coffin, opting for the pink tie & gray suit, i felt that the grimness we felt need not be communicated. in my childhood i spent some time trying to comprehend what was happening. i'd lie on the bed, tracing

the patterns of the bedspread's design, never succeeding. i needed assistance. i
became a very serious person.

june 21, oh oh 2020 it's fuckin father's day, a free ice cream cone from moxie's,
hot as hell climate change heat, coronavirus time, trump had a rally in tulsa,
we saw a mink in the backyard, also a jackrabbit, today annabel will come,
hard to believe anybody will come, the birds nesting on the back porch, enter-
ing through the screens are, according to phil via sibley's, house wrens! perhaps
it came from the other porch, a worm-eater, if you will; we also have warblers,
sweet singers all. here a spider eating a caterpillar, a good meal for both dad &
grads.

From All Sides

her hand's on her hip
she looks, maybe down
the window trembles

she looks down while
the window trembles
but she's become a tree
out of her head comes
a tree that begins at the roof
safest place to be is the past

Star Wars

Everybody knows
you said that night
"I like you both so much
why don't we all sleep together?"
I can't remember
if it was before or after
you said that I thought
you were just tired
& I offered you the couch
you said "I don't wanna sleep
on the couch at all!"
you brave person
you say you can't remember
now none of us can remember
what day that was
& I've no idea how many times
we've slept together so far
sleeping together is a weird phrase
this whole liaison could be just a phase
some one of us thinks or says
we're all poets
you're the most lighthearted
except no that's not so
I'm full of psychology
we all meditate and brood
on the roof in bed over supper
or wherever we can weep or eat
I can't remember what world
we are living in anymore
I remember Freud nearsighted
mentioning sex will be sublimated
so it may be this part of art
when you got mad at Lewis

for wanting to fuck me
right after you had made me come
you smoked a cigarette
& I said Lewis you're greedy
this was nice religious sex
where you stop sex for a while
and talk about religion
we had toyed with the idea
of dressing up as priests & nuns
we thought for your poster for your reading
Lewis could be the priest hearing your confession
he'd be naked except for his collar
& you but for your fantastic headdress
in a cut-out confessional like a movie set
do you think we're all scared
you can't remember the time
you fell asleep while I made love to you
I hope it didn't seem like
I didn't like your house
because I was allergic to the cat
when we walked around that day
our children adopted your hands
& we'd talked about all moving in
to your place, saving lots of money on rent
& getting a place in the country
living like Chinese communists
in your cheaper apartment
always together
writing the three of us in one room
on pads in longhand on our knees
as if our poems were like scrubbing floors
which they are always
we could take turns adjourning
to the roof in the balmier seasons
one of us awkwardly left behind with the children
our love then is economic besides religious

but it's a secret what would the Schneemans
the Padgetts the Berrigan-Notleys think
we don't want to be available
to other men and women as a result
of our love we wouldn't want the project
to be affected by it nevertheless
we want to shout all about it
though none of us knows what will come of it
when you walk down the street in, say, New England
with two or three children people often smile
approvingly, even in New York that happens
even today that happened to you with our children
in your tow as they say while I was in the store
what did you think of that
how come then all this is not as acceptable as that
I know you know the answer but don't say it yet
when we first made love we were not at all confused
after that sometimes one of us would feel left out
I see this can't be the subject of a poem
because it has nothing to do with others
but the Eskimos
and some others nobody knows
what will happen next I can't remember
I only wish next was always sooner
in our etiquette which is a ticket
that sticks to nobody in all this
you have birds in your apartment at one end
you are lucky as the cat comes in
when you make love to me we are independent
I can't say that I'd better call you up
aw shit you aren't home
if this poem becomes a 77-page poem
what'll happen by the end of it
it could be a semi-fictitious narrative
in which we become like others
I sit around thinking

about anything, everything in the papers
seems to have something to do with me
with us there is always this problem of the news
what would you think about exactly what
I'm reading about
Often I've no idea
I know I'll be sorry for writing this poem
if it is a poem
but I couldn't stop speaking
but that doesn't mean it's sublimation
but if you'd been here I wouldn't have
written this in these lines but I'd have
tried to tell as much as I could
between our taking turns
paying attention too to the parts of our forms
already done & used in time for this pleasure
not as one in this particular instance as they say
but us others all vying for sweet conduct
through a proliferation of love
you generously & bravely began
though you can't remember you did
so it's a lucky thing there were witnesses
like at the family table nobody in the world
would remember but every poet might write
if she or he were of the school or community
where it's okay to say whatever the hell you want
including being narcissistic which you thought you were
but I must admit you weren't
and now how am I going to end this
I've got to mention secrecy again
oh just to say if we can say anything
I still promise this poem still had to be written
where I could say anything I wanted to
to you my lover my colleague my daughter & sister
& for our lover my lover my father & brother
on the way out traveling with the red & blue lights

& all the way back coming home
or else I'd go mad cause I couldn't write
anything about what I was thinking about
all this time an eternity if you'll forgive me
between our getting back together like a journey
& nobody knows except for Grace & Peggy & your sister
& why if we were like the people in the pictures
of our families would we expect anybody
to ever know about our love
all unusual like another family scandal
reported once by people looking at picture books
as a thing that happened around 1981
among two crazy aunts and an uncle, each by someone
who loves to remember everything
but for them, they'll have our poems
if they'll be as clear as any night is to us.

Absence of Faces

when no figures appeared
absolutized by a form of love
the non-something of transforming
an enclave of what they call
straight lines—they would be lost
is lost false? in almost anywhere else
i'd say to you i know
i'd draw people to our not drawn breath
overpriced & dramatic dried flower
let me see
i will not show them to you
there was the miracle of his not permitting the sight
      of the numbering, the pre-arranged one
      was/is only a form of innocence, i mean
      influence, we talked about colors &
      there's the hiking & hitchhiking rainbow
      family, the haunted-house display
is the work to be done in secret or out loud?
all wait for your worry in the central part of it
as we've learned from concept art
from reading 21st century magazines
no one can
not begin again
write a beautiful elegant version of this
no i can't say this

it's sort of raining. everything's wet. it rained all day, now it is so dark, it's a simple thought: in catastrophes the best & most mutual-aidish is brought out in people—who needs governments. some mistake was once made that we need leaders! leaders lead to monuments & they just have to be taken down. the future's more in the past but what is this that's happening now? the rain it raineth every day & it will never stop, this will be good for the tomatoes, just above the bird feeder is blue sky, now thunder, no rainbows though

Wandering Scholars

some such sum or sun
something similar like what we seek
when in poorer dresses left behind
like the profligate trees even kinder to the poor
though they have to pay with their cars
we cast out on this rigid trip to live in the city
again as once when our arms when we walked were more free

a generation later the water power or pressure
stops as it often did then, a child or children look
and you fear from being tied they will fall
in the moat at the zoo where the swans swim in
shallow white water painted blue, a whistle takes place
and in the corridors behind the big house bottles break
it is a symphony of what is liked to be being done by
someone around here, maybe many more, this anachronistic place

that wasn't memory dear derogated word of inexacting
limits to the cheerful or awful as you like it often as good
as Twelfth Night then as bad, which baby cries, as any of the tragedies

xeroxing is as available as the recurring disco radio,
both act as a mind to reproduce the weary torsos of the poems
and of the discoettes not always punk some more so than
the woman with partly purple hair on the bus with her mother,
what ineluctable public education was the kindly mother getting
while the cared-for toes of the other travelers signaled some
form of custom the battered feet of the meter opposite had ignored

it's a little too complicated to go into if you don't feel free
or have the energy to raise the roof of the rented rooms
the poetry seems written like the yardage on the fabric of a curtain—
if you chose to leave it out without a hand-sewn hem you might wind up

craving a character in error like the volunteering clowns in the park
who wish to be discovered but only embarrass the children
with their overwrought ambitions to Shakespearean memories of
light like the lights of a new set of rooms, one too
bright one too yellow one a depressing fluorescent to cook under
all the foods of Naples Florence the Ukraine Lithuania & Warsaw
mixed together in a kind of sleep soup which expects the dream of all
the clownish moving to be recurring because a symptom of the reason
of our east coastern civilization where the housing is uncertain
of its normal claims for shelter and to provide water
& light like the light of any light under which or by we might
write poetry not only makes us silly though we crave a formidable exemp-
tion
but makes for silly poetry like the addled unhomogenized dinner I
made you my friends my guests whom and the free rooms
of all the parts of the city I had studied like poetry's history
I loved and returned to. I left a perfectly good piece of equipment
behind under a bush. But I got away so what does it matter?
Let it go, I can find another one equally good here.

i'm bored to tears, the weather is warm. i've moved my operation off the porch;
it was a cold day, it's sort of raining, we saw a brilliantly red tree in rayville,
everything on my piles falls down into hades, i'd better empty out hell & use it
as a storage bin so i have room to type. there's stinkbugs everywhere. tonight
we'll go to an ashbery memorial. to know where everything is to be at last
alone. but who wants that? a scintillating set-to, or a being-here, or a being-
here. not growing old gracefully, i've chosen to grow old awkwardly, like a
teenager. i don't want anyone to know i'm here. it's dark & unsavory where
i go but i never go, i never went, through the window headfirst, imminent
somersaulting by the door, i can't hear you, i need an ear-horn. i'm a katydid
in distress.

we are covered with a cloud that makes it rain on us during this, oh, pandemic
time, the eve of july, is this a disaster? problem is, it has no end. it's a tedious
story, i've told it a million times. i think you could call this a disaster, yes you
could, beulah.

july 2, memory is running, that's the only july i remember, i mean that july
is the only, are the only things i remember, don't have time for more, i mean
room, red sorrel, popover, joel schumacher, time is a room, you could say time
was anything; about MEMORY, stop time is a curtain blowing in the wind, i
remember what's in the pictures but not what's in the words, the words could
be any words, maybe i should've memorized memory.

these rich areas of thought & time

in case memory might mention poetry that's
spoken for, fractions of pages flying off like
fractions of brandy still left in the bottle of
some future spitting out hay into bales, not
rolls, how far is harlemville from cooperstown, i'm
so old now. concentration's slower like my eyes look
out & the rest of me's behind them, the tedder's
done. does erudition have a luster? is the
sublime edible like viper's bugloss? a full blast
of sun is on the shirt on a hanger, here comes
myself, walking down the street saying "neckerchief,
handkerchief," that's all, with a camera on her
hip in a full blast of sun, dressed in white like
the universe spiced with entropy, your imagined
lightning & my reflected sound, close as a sleeping
sail

this is june 26 maybe, a murky sunday

this disastrous time, well this isn't exactly a disaster, it's i don't know what-chamacallit, isn't that a bklyn term?

i guess the birds don't know the grass is taller than they are.

Untitled

Hear the thrusts, deaths, and sighs,
or was each a soul scream
heart-rending at its heart
and horrible.

Is the sigh the soul
or does it drink only lightly at the top
like bees from water?

Do the words come through
piercing, who did it—
(does the bird touch his flight,
feeling free, out of rule)?

Are he and the things of him one,
or do they start stop fast
now one now him.

Is he dead thinking
sweet is the joy I long for
or forced stopped thinking
in the cool green rot of his body?

Does he faint
can he hear his own sigh
is it shorter than it sounds,
ring or rattle, clear through
down the bones.

At the moment then the thing
pure death comes
has he gone, did it touch
is it clear then

or will all pass by
without sense and what's above
yes and no
and why ask (how) is it thinking
that we die with nothing or with all
and why

Heart

A slip of the tongue
Between my legs

children are screeching at the swimming hole near the hiking trail. today we're having the great handover of unpasteurized milk for lydia from sarah, all done maintaining the social distancing rules. people will forget how much they like each other.

july 3rd, assistant to the birds, bernadette mayer. this pandemic thing is never going to end unless we just don't care if we get sick or not, i just ate five shrimp, none of what i wrote makes sense, it won't end then at all, just get worse so you could say if you don't care if it's hot or cold.

I Am Your Food I Am Your Fate

something's in the oven we've got so much to do
I always say one thing when I mean to say two
do you love me do you think me the densest aristocrat
who ever spoke to you in rhymes when the rates were flat

is your heart right here & am I your best bet
do you want a beer do you want a cigarette
I know you think I have a lot of really bad habits
but my love for you multiplies just like rabbits

I sit in my room at my appointed time
and I wonder about words and I wonder about rhyme
and then I think I'd better fix it so we can make some money
but I only wind up fixing up me and you, honey

in my poems I like to talk about what happens in my heart
and I know I'm cold and selfish but it's part of the art
of learning to know that my world won't go away
it's behind me every night it's before me every day

we start and we stop, there's an awful lot to do
we begin to say one thing and we wind up saying two
I might say I love you I might mean to grab your guy
when before I can do it there's some juice in my eye

I wonder what will happen when we get to be forty-three
do you think you'll still love me as I will still love thee?
Marie will be twelve then and Sophia will be ten
here's all my love for now & here it is again for then

Pi-Day

                        you are an unending
                        decimal—you see?

no matter how many
                        b&w paramount movies you see
                                        that are risqué
        things will come in
                        to sweep & vacuum-clean
        everywhere
                        even under the table
cleaning by
                a decimal animal
                                whenever you don't
                notice
                please let us
                                stand on a chair
        to
        give a speech
                        each of your hairs
                                        says
I am within
                the realm
                        of figuring out
how everybody twinkles
                        on this day
                                        like clouds
                thru icicles
                                ground covered
        with snow
                        how could this be?
        how many pies
                        can we eat?

                    birthday is pi-day, yay
            "you have the pi-day powers"

you know   it's showering
                                icicles & drops
                everything
                        on
                            everybody

the woman across the road, alice zachariewicz, has put up a sign: welcome to gethsemane hill. oh what did i do to deserve this in my old age? we even had to put up a curtain so we couldn't see it all the time.

it is 4th of july, a nothing
4th, the pandemic 4th, no reading
of the whole truth this year
snap & crackle go the tree
half of the deer blind
fell taking over the whole
forest, dividing it in half
enough wood for the whole winter
if you measure the winter in wood
it fell on july 4th, no reading
of the whole truth this year, I
saw a whole circle of pinks

it's wednesday july 8. if you leave DON'T GO TO LA! or below, everybody's either being shot or has the coronavirus & now it's july 9th, the hottest day in the world, gee not much happens in a day, eh? should i really say july 11 on the same page? who'm i asking?

apparently more than one place in the world says it has had the first free lending library. I found "being and time" under the table. ancient ontology: we all have our moments under the table. some bang their heads. at times a needed bang. you have to have everything you need with you, in case you can't get it, like a pinking shears. but not a bang.

Don't Forget Volcanic Salt

Too cold for prosciutto, too cold for seltzer
two eyes black, one eye green
too cold for ice cubes, I have an eye for cubes
a head for new pillows and old antifreeze
a lookout for reflections of light above red flowers
baseless are the flowers that fly like humans
in through the window that looks out on nothing
nowhere near the volcanoes of the world
there's a ring of fire and eternal springtime
we force the bulbs to produce flowers out of season
one amaryllis wafts to give a shadow to the salt
but the paper is clean as an ideal window, it's cold
bare ruined choirs the trees, but the snow is fake
the war on winter weather warms indoor plants
artificial northern light display at the ready
new leaves give shock to old people
if I remember it right, amaryllis equals hibiscus

All the zingers boiled up in a cup
steam for the dry air around here
as someone forgets to measure shadows
shadows are unboiled zingers like when
you go swimming in the lake near a dock
and look like a monster in the afternoon
they lurk on pages between leather covers
we cover our skin with fibers some made from plants
people gather around fires and put ice in their drinks
or a coil that warms it up, remember those? soon
we can't remember what should be cold or hot
like a hot shower suddenly interrupted by your hand
you meant well but only the ice glistens
and the fire talks to Bernadette behind her back
it goes like popcorn at the million dollar movie

it shines like a greenhouse in the sunset
or a rainbow in the middle of the forest
we bottle sunshine for the next grim day
we put it in the creeks for safekeeping
the sale price is overwhelming; it's out of reach

the way ducks fly upriver and float downstream
or strange formations in the sky accent the day
the way Mergansers go against the tide
but wait! the sun came out for a second, o sun
get to your seat! you must not move—you moved!

WITH PHILIP GOOD, FEBRUARY '22

The Lobelias of Fear

there are maple trees, one, two, three
but wait there's 5 more, 2 behind the bungalow
and lots in the poetry state forest
I hear target practice from far away, it's
probably for shooting deer, bears and dinosaurs
but how will we, still alive, socialize
in the winter? wrapped in bear skins
we'll sit around pot-bellied stoves eating
the lobelias of fear left over from desperation
last summer's woodland sunflowers and bee balm
remind us of black cherry eaten in a hurry
while the yard grows in the moonlight
shrinking like a salary or a damaged item
when we return in the morning for a breakfast
of harvest petunias sprinkled with wild marsh mallow

No More Reading

"spending most of its life
in a solera"

Except in the middle of the night
These fucking flies too half-dead to buzz off
I think we are classicists nonetheless
But we have too much to do
Too much history to put into poetry
Too much time to age the prose
In oak casks till it withers the line
I didn't spend my life timed like frost so far
Figuring out anything all wrong in pounds
We put babies to bed, they don't stay there either
Water comes up through the sink instead of going down
It's cold but it hasn't killed us yet
It's a classic traditional October
I have no sense of humor
About the unrelenting beauty of all these leaves
When I recover I'll make a list
Of things to do when I feel better
First, look at all the rhymes I've missed so far
Song with wrong, neither with either
Not frown with down but maybe brown or uptown
Then with yet the Anglo-Saxon get
Or the Greek alphabet, then I'm doing something
Like looking up etymologies and meanings in a book
Makes you more respectable than just some crook
Lighting matches one-handed in a sinister alley
Cynically stealing though words from a movie
The humor of October's leaves and trees
Could go with divorcees or the Maccabees
So split and turned we'd rather make a fist

And fight it out in person or by letter
Prose goes with rose & pope's nose & clothes
Gertrude Stein was really fat, how about that
Let's be patriots too, hammer all the heads into hearts,
Some hearts to heads, that's the trouble
With all false poetic starts, wholes for parts
Or parts wholes, also I have a double
An imposter, she writes so I can forget
Everything even the rudimentary English alphabet
Yet I still put time in on this dopey rhyming
At the expense of looking at erudite books
Ruder still I forget love can kill
But the only time I'm letting myself be forgetting
This loving kiss of everything memory too
Is when I'm writing or we're fighting
Or who I am not only then, my love, loves you

The Cactus Is Flowering

We were having trouble with all the people
      and firecrackers
One man forgot you couldn't do anything but
      write poetry
And otherwise you just had to sleep and stay
      still in your bed
Another said it was the man of action that might
      only write
Somebody had a party to which hardly anybody
      was invited
We couldn't get inspired to keep our house in
      order this year
The house was a mess and we went to bed too late
      to fix it up
We'd lost our old way of thinking where we knew
      what to do next
We got scared and figured we were just one of
      the cactuses will flower
Couldn't hang up the laundry couldn't wash it
      couldn't get up the street
Took no pleasure in the kind of way the heat
      was increasing this spring
Felt as if we were at a bar drinking all the
      time we were thinking
Lost progress we'd already made like in a
      scientific experiment
Made everyone laugh at us and think we were
      pitiable and old, regressing
Couldn't figure out the news, hadn't the energy
      to amuse our parents, be sprightly
I think we needed a spring tonic or to be reminded
      of old-fashioned spring water

Or something, we even forgot what world we lived in
        we couldn't sleep on any porch
We slept in old beds never made up for lack of time
        we stopped answering the phone
Once in a while one of two poets would smile at us
        in such a way as to make us remember
How we were supposed to be & what way to be &
        what it felt like to be that way
And we began to hope that over the summer we could
        get back to the lost minion
Or else we'd be bad, lost and not good, done in,
        without love & dead

the flies are award-winning today, the birds did that thing where they fly thru the air, eating insects, it's crazy, it makes you think of the end of the world, which if it was wouldn't involve eating insects but maybe it would for us humans, we'd open our mouths in awe at what was happening & in would fly the flies, spiders, bees, moths, replicators, ants, flying beetles & cockroaches, walking sticks but they don't fly, dreaming walking sticks.

this journal is as confused, mixed up, as this time is—imagine trying to represent not knowing whether there's school in the fall or if there are tests: the "president" has sent troops to cities with democratic mayors to quell the demonstrations about all the black people cops have shot & killed in other ways, he will most likely declare martial law thinking thereby he can stay president even if he's not elected. in the field are patches of wild thyme or oregano, me, i mistype a lot of things, misheard black cherry as raspberry, wishful thinking.

now the leaves are rushing off the yellow tree, yeller gal, yeller gal, flashing through the night, summer storms will pass you, unless the lightning's white. but that was an airplane. my favorite thing to do is to watch a volcano erupt or see the northern lights. i'd like to have seen the nazca lines & everything in asia, i'd like to have gone to madagascar, i'd like to go to the botanical gardens in lesotho. i'd like to see the glass flowers in boston & i may yet. if we're going to skip seasons, let's have it be spring, 60°, perpetual like periwinkles. there's no reason it couldn't be like that here, now, you know? we wouldn't have to theorize about why. & the deer ticks would be gone. no one would know where they went, but the deer would still be around. there's a bear around near here; there must be confusion about hibernation.

unconditional death is a good title because it's almost completely meaningless, yes? i wrapped the green tomatoes in newspaper, rolled up the lovage in wet paper towels, mailed peggy's postcard, didn't see the bear, emptied the sink, read rebecca solnit, said to the greens "would anybody like to go to gethsemane hill with me? i have to atone for my sins." thought about ball lightning, thought that it's friday & about the s&s brewery in nassau. when there's a frost, do the poison plants die?

My Parents' Politics

there's a long list of unbelievability between the list
of the loss of my watch and what they did to me
they said but I can't say it
i know this now & i can say this now that they would be
in favor of the uno govt of nicaragua or else
very confused by the misuse of their pension funds
i know they would be looking askance at me for my
amazement at the cruelty of humans
a cruelness they themselves had contributed to through
their initiated greed within the fault of the arctic
of the brand-new everything
frozen foods were new to my mother so i forgive her
i myself am stupid exactly because she was so
it can be proven—we looked we enjoyed at the t.v.
on birthdays we ate breyers ice cream before the performances of the
    republicans
the thing i'm trying to say is we hated what capitalism
brought us even in the early fifties
when i was six and i saw my father fight with others
about what to watch on t.v.

i spit on them for not knowing not counting up how it could
become the dumb future of capitalism, they watched
ronald reagan on the g.e. show knowing full well
nothing, my father couldn't work with the union
he said it was corrupt (why doesn't john ask berry)
machine i know not what you do

i am suddenly going and i care not what you do
i just want to find out more about how humans
can start a fight with others, i spit on literature
it's taken me long enough, you spit on it too
i encourage you.

i hate my father & mother whom i loved
for contributing to fuck god nothing the fucking above
i cannot say what i don't know but darling
they seem to have ruined love & hope
with their dumb specific greed
i do not give up—

I Am Taken about Your Actual Fish

to me it is more golden
than an aurora of sparkling green
the green of the field
now does not compare
if i were to eat something now
it would be a 4-layer cake with raspberries and cream
or perhaps a lemon cake
with the same adornments
but also blackberries

for me, to eat has been
ruined by the catholic church
for that "host" to be a body
& then to swallow it
is enough to ruin swallowing
& hunger forever, mr. jesus christ
especially when your servants
put their cocks in my mouth

The Breadth of or Homage to a Frozen Waterfall

Without recourse to thought I'd like to say
it gives to the hearth like bread a something
& in a tiny Tom & Jerry jelly glass becomes the
great blue ice that could permit us to continue on
i won't tell you why but if you could only see it!
where's a moment? we are done for!
the bath of idiocy that precedes us to the waterfall
if anyone goes there, makes us doubt the pretty semolina
the vaginas, not to discount the penises that precede us there
on that route there is only one man who says, no kidding
"you are going to have a hard time crossing that stream"
or else he says "wow cool how are you planning to cross
that stream; I myself went over on a fallen log
& came back in these boots—he held them up as an
emblem as if to say, holy shit there is a lot to be spoken
about and certainly a lot to be done unnoticed in this
world
implying of all the lyrical it's like when people get
older
the trial is to steal youth somehow
or to close the piano till the only player in the house
comes home or to cease saying things that even sound like
metaphors—wow what a conundrum—that means we don't know
if we're here or there
all mixed up in our society at least you are

anyway this waterfall was blatantly blue and if you look it up
that means also yellow & black which means white yet it
was blue to the look

sunday's always this stupid day, always's always between sundays & this unless it relates to a different day (of the week), sundays relate to stupidity, no matter how you think of them, & it is sunday but now it doesn't even matter because it is this day because i'm here. could the memory of sun, if it were strong enough, make you warm? what about going to sleep by keeping your thoughts inside the brain, not in the outside world? the world beyond the noggin? there is a coast along the inside that doesn't allow for the stuff that keeps you awake, it's kind of too simple. simple monday, washing day, school day, another sunny day but cold.

today wildfires are still burning, the pandemic's not ended but it isn't winter yet, there'll be a few 70° days this week.

now it's weirdly warm again, turns me from my purpose, i'm stalled, but what's my purpose? it is fall but so far a cold fall, now with air from the western fires making everything a weird color.

the sun's come out! now the sky's even weirder but yellow trees look yellower (rewolley) it's even yellow backwards. the birds have been slow to know there's seed in the feeder, I feel. I thought I saw an elephant. the leaves've stopped falling for a day, a skinny-leafed branch waving in the wind looks like an extraterrestrial, just like me. humans & other mammals have ancient viruses in their bodies, some think to keep mothers from eating their children. or maybe they could be extraterrestrial ingredients, so that life could occur.

Simon's in China
Because but Yet or Still Again

I have a craving to write
To someone who loves me without reserve
So it's switched into my poems
To want to be loved all the time I think
Of why the children take so long
To want it like children like a party
Where we're celebrating anything
Just like children at a party
Like women and also like ice
Like luxuriant hair or like a crew cut
And then they grow to love
And to steal or pretend they steal
From love what love was or what they will
They didn't take my good pens after all
I had a dream about poets in an inky pool
Like Dante, more or less like love
Like beer on the frozen windowsill
Where the cold comes in but not the air
Like a silver hair, like romance, an idea
Of being adored and caressed, a need
In harsh stolen solitude this midwinter,
That kind of love and every other kind
What was my dream, who were its followers
Old morning, old warning of beauty,
Fear of love, I do not feel cold
Romance was once a luxury, now it's hard
To abjure this winter, even harder
To be so solemn about the weather
I think I'll forget my dream
And also all my promises and images
There are some things you can only put
One way, others a different way each time,

It doesn't matter, I'll wait around out of habit
Considering this a luxury and that a hard stone
Loving you as if I were walking sensationally
Down the stairs looking fast or else
Running up a bill still smiling at the store
Without a thought to the consequent past.

after my parents died i was adopted by jeanne moreau & henry david thoreau,
two assiniboine indians who taught me what really happened in history. it was
good at last to know & speak my own language. when lewis's mother went to
hunter high school, they made her take a class to get rid of her yiddish accent.
who decides you shouldn't have one?

i dreamt i was a pinnacle of coral.

the thought of what america would be like if the classics had a wide circula-
tion, the thought of what america blah blah, bitter america, it's the beginning
of 70 degree days ending in rain, a lot of people would die of the virus quoting
herodotus or maybe sappho, the greek anthology. americans are a bit anti-in-
tellectual. even politicians don't quote poetry anymore, though obama was a
reader.

the idea that writing is easy comes from the frank o'hara method. but it is in
fact easy, especially if you don't try to say more than you are thinking, to say
other than what you're thinking, for instance you might be trying to say what
somebody else is thinking, like barthes or lacan. slowly does the middle tree
turn yellow, always having been the most interesting fall tree, it is somewhat
damaged with dead parts you can see from the field, it's the tree whose branch
snapped off & hung there threatening our (covid) social life till when it fell.
now threatening is cold weather, can't sit outdoors, our plan is to borrow a tent
from grace, & in it use our mr. heater buddy, little buddy, maybe it will work

today's monday august 31, oh fuck, though the sun is out, it's foreboding, don't
think about it, thinking about the future's outlawed esp. if you're 75 & human,
we sat in the sun with alyssa & finally everyone, in the field before us a horse, a
bit skittish, the kids took no notice, surprisingly, it was an odd sight to be sure.

maybe it's just fear of the winter, this is a day supposed to be sunny but what
is this white sky? seen some yellow & orange trees, the sky is white: western
wildfires, we're having a drought.

so many leaves are
falling, it's exhausting

To Sophia

Now finally I've gotten to the bottom of it
I've got a few minutes left to tell the story of it
I gently wake myself up every day in the same delicate kind of dream's
    moment
Doesn't everybody wake up sometime to say
Don't bother me again just yet and how did I wind up here
I know it's not poetry to say so but how
Did I wind up having to move into another room to write another book
And while moving everything to have to study all the old things I've kept,
    endless negatives and slides held up to the light with friends and trees
    and families on them
So many papers and even some checks, old tapes with another voice of
    mine
Exhaustion's neighbor memory keeps telling me what I used to think then I
    still think
Now nostalgia for a tree makes me dally at the identifying window
I'm donating to you, younger daughter, I'm one or was one
You need to sleep alone
Away from the exotic noisy sleep of groaning parents
Who don't even know what they do or say in their sleep
You need to drink thought more privately
And not awaken every night in the same energetic need
To be comforted and nursed like a baby

Sophia you can have my old dark room of wars
I'm moving my desk to Main Street to work under the lights
Watch out for the rising moon, the looming eastern stars
Let's exchange the awful peace of our nights

Untitled

I write my poems with my hands on my breasts
smelling the redolent smells of all the lilacs I can get
for whatever occasion of appropriate love
I walk through the woods wondering about sex
I walk through the city craving the Indian men and
the Korean women & the Japanese women & the white men too
I don't mean to pretend to be Walt Whitman but I do
desire you with eyes and possibly heart only
and when you kiss me which I crave I only occasionally
feel the rest, many of us have to live without beauty
of the traditional sorts of hearts, we are millions of people
just as earnest in our beings and skins as everyone

at last the sun appears. it's the "last" sunny day before 5 days of rain. the frequency of rain because of global warming—all those words are all wrong— seems too right, as if the atmosphere needed to be washed.

there's two tiny potatoes on my desk. sounds of the speedway in earshot.

this is the weirdest sunday: the road is wet, the clouds are dark, some trees turning somewhat yellow, saw two stinkbugs on the window, all bugs are over- producing but the gingko tree hasn't done any of its autumn tricks yet.

in the middle of the night, the "imp" would come, dangers of going to the cellar, turning on the light, now i think i can never have to do that again, write it down "expressively" whatever that means, it means the same thing as index- icality i guess, i'm throwing you away forever, not to make a big deal of it, remember barbara barb's magazine or barbara something's "big deal," there's water in the birdbath & the birds are thirsty, the birds are being feisty, who else is feisty & thirsty? me? maybe.

june 13 what time is it? it's around aster time, the beginning of aster time, just past iris time, saturday, the day to chase birds from the front porch, maybe, to walk by the kinderhook creek, phil's putting more soil in the fig plant which could go either way—life or death or bungalow. life, death, or the bungalow. front porch birds, still don't know. wrens, warblers, other? bees, bramble bushes in bloom (it's their birthday), airplanes, heard 2, & a meal to go last night, zuppa di pesce & pork saltimbocca, it's cold for this june, excursion to dump, was it a joyride? the smell of joy accompanied us to the dump but, oddly, it didn't come back with us like a grandmother. statues of slave owners are being removed, maybe too all those signs that say "george washington slept here"

Three Envelopes

I put the bad guys on one side
and the good guys on the other side for today
On the bad side's the Hand Rehabilitation Services and Bush
On the good side's St. Luke's and Dukakis
The bad side wants money over everything or power maybe
The good side cares about people's ways of being
Add they don't want nothing but
They understand the concept of it
The bad side said to my son Max, "We don't
Care for your healing unless the giant
Bill is paid," so I have a feeling to say to the bad side
"This is my darling you'd better
help yourself to loving him cause otherwise,
Cocksucker motherfucker infant-tormentor
You already have wound up in the most dismal
Circles of hell that can be dreamed of
        PLUS therefore, fuck you"

Art Has Lapsed We Know

Art has lapsed we know since nothing's
happening but the poet's free dream
in the rich hands of exhaustion of who
to invite the lover or the lover?

This is not to speak
This is not said to speak
We are not speaking now, we were
never speaking

For what succeeds is silly maybe
For what succeeds is maybe silly
There might be nostalgia, emotion
There might be stuff unknown as death
Let something something something
Please, let something something something

Dead Is the Dumb Ass Lover

No not dead is the dumb ass lover who
Watches nothing ever, thee is the saint of
like-politics and as such exists not in words
since here is nothing that is something in a
Venetian blind or funny cover of crap designed
to be over the twelfth the eleventh, the present
century or what, you can't say that, besides tomorrow
You won't even be here or at the Cloisters so
Forget dreams, living one of somewhere
And try and just stay here, change plans,
Make new ones, don't go to work, stay home stay

Mean Times

Was I wrong to speak in thought
So brain (not speech) of spring?

Did any slightest city notice
What I'd learned of your nice devouring?

& did the mayor then by my acutest love
Reform the inexact & unfair rent laws?

& did the school board at last give the lie
To their cruel & wintry recidivist bureaucracy?

Did a cup of bitter coffee on Avenue A
Get somewhat closer to being almost free?

& did the bitter president suddenly decide
American humans could legally be loving?

& did the other so-called heads of inaccurate states
Fall down in misery at their all kinds of greed
To resurrect a beautiful way of being honest
Spiritual & subservient to the thought (not speech)
Of the exactest the most complex the good of all?

Did men & women learn to have two voices
Unequivocal amidst the nature of things?

Of course they all did all this then & thus
A rewriting of the formerly fatherly tables
Took place at my look at you just past
The vernal equinox of this sidereal day
(Equal to 23 hours, 56 minutes and
4 & 9/100ths seconds of mean solar time).

it's like in the next line i'll really show that wherever in the midst of the pandemic, there's vaccines; just past thanksgiving & xmas, with virus spreading haywirishly, can i come to your house?

here were the mahican indians, but tsatsawassa is german too, cup of water. all around tsatsawassa lake's private property, you can't swim in it or at least newcomers can't but i don't think even oldcomers can except the people who live right on, in front of, the lake because it's so dangerous or something. i hope the tsatsawassa lake monster comes soon to eat them, then let us swim. new lebanon, the town we pay school taxes to, was the site of the first free library in the u.s. lebanon is also the site of the first thermometer & barometer factories & the first pharmaceutical firm (for medicinal plant remedies). could any of this be true?

soon it'll be even darker than it already is. alice, our neighbor across the road, has put up a sign, it says "gethsemane hill" no, it says "welcome to gethsemane hill." i don't think anyone is ever welcomed there, it's where christians believe jesus christ was crucified. if you go up the hill, alice has made the stations of the cross which are like dioramas where you stop & meditate on suffering. i forget what they all are.

it's tuesday, there was something important to say here now but i can't remember what part of the future it was. so bear with me—will the pink leaves darken or will they become orange? purple? something else? & if you turn them over, a whole different kind of color maybe. what's the color look like you can't see? tell us, they'll banish us you know.

when will we get to the meat of this thing? well this is a vegetarian thing. leonardo was too, i am not but this is. but the meat in supermarkets is often old & smelly like onions, sometimes the library. those purple berries are good for ink but don't drink them. there's a lot of nightshade on staten island, so it won't change the world but will espouse a theory of everything beginning in pink & ending up something else like we're pretending there is a place to start & end like a meal, some meals have no end unless you fall down on your knees propped up by your elbows, it's amazing how long we can talk about ordinary everyday things like the way you touched the clothes that had been cleaned, while folding them like a derringer. as i am on this porch, i'm in between life, which is behind me & the field which is a stage hardly anyone enters left or right, so now i can say i'm busy like the rest of us, sitting here between the sun & the darkness, it could be of the past or the future, what say you? a field guide to feathers is on my birthday list. I think m is confused because you are both so anxious for her to be either when it goes without saying we probably have a choice, but who cares? you can still love ants.

dec. 21 it's the real midwinter day today, the shortest day of the year seeming like the longest
they were discussing all the different doorbells & asked the salesperson to
CHIME IN
oh well

walked out onto the back porch, instantly remembered this light, the light of after a lot of leaves have fallen. talked on the phone with sophie, lewis seems to be dying, is on opioids, i, alive, have shallots & scallops for lunch, the shallots are unbelievably great, i am unbelievably narcissistic, read the rest of count luna this morning, it's all about death, i don't know how to behave when somebody's dying, never did, never will, maybe i will when i'm the one dying, it'll be easier maybe, fallen leaves on the tent,

tuesday october 6, 2020, it's 67° 67° even just being in florida seems like disaster there was supposed to be 50-mile-an-hour wind to scare us today but so far not, it's gray, the tent is falling down & the winter finches are around. i read "the story of english" & the word "gullah" puts me in a fugue state.

On the Wild Strawberry

Does every flower mean a fruit?
if so, the ones near the well will
make more than my annual handful

If I were organized and fastidious
I'd tie a red string to every flower so
I'd know and could brag that a naked plant

Fed me a good dessert

from *The Second World of Nature*
or
Next Planet

why are the leaves just pink, why will i have to go inside when it freezes instead of just living on the fortunate isles?

it's more like dec 10th & what a stupid time it is! pandemic worse than ever, nobody, including me, knows what they are doing, or am i male or female.

THE SKY IS WHITE, CLOUDS IN REVERSE, an archetypal october day, many people died today, some of coronavirus, some in the war of armenia & ajerbaijan, some in wars in the middle east, we went to get birdseed at ocean state, my first trip out into the world of the infected.

it's a bright gray sky, no frosts in sight, it's odd out, injustice is being done, some blue seen, injustice still being done, but the sun! injustice is being overrun by the sun, today is tuesday october 20, oh no, that's the worst day in the history of days, it's hardly lucky, maybe round, it's the day my father died, it's time to forget these ancient horrors. this day is a day when the clouds are bright.

IT IS AUG & A MONDAY, oops aug 17 i keep feelin i'm losing my mind, i'm sure a lot of minds are being lost these days

what should i do now? it's tuesday, everybody thinks too much & doesn't know how to write the thinking down, though they want to. as for me, i don't know what to have for breakfast. i don't go out because of the ticks.

i'm old enough to drink! if i were to be able to choose anything to eat in the whole world, i think i'd have an ethiopian lunch eaten with my hands & fingers like a lobster's claws

the gingko tree is leafless, there's a coyote sound around, haven't heard it since pre-lawn days here. nabokov remembers his future works! at last somebody besides whales. i'm reading "insomniac dreams" in which he's keeping a dream record to try to prove dunne's theory that dreams are precognitive. there is talk of time travel too. read "the gift" and the fourth part of "ada." HE SAYS HE SEEMS TO REMEMBER THEM. GUESS EVERYBODY then was afraid of seeming crazy(?) except dunne. the sun is out. for nothing to be on the paper is a coyote, a guy shot a giant bear after falling out of a tree stand. i wonder if there are a lot of people in loony bins who remember the future(?) today? in the past? in the future? i see a fly, i saw a fly, i will see a fly, i fell on a saw, no, it was a seesaw. there's stinkbug on my goldenrod paper. oh my. oh geez.

the beginning's not the start, the end's not the finale, like they say & the middle, it's not equidistant from the start & end, like if you're a middle child you don't always come between the first & last children, there would be half-children anywhere or fractions of children all about lying like firecrackers on the sidewalk waiting to explode or crack so you mean if i got bottom teeth would i then be covered? from what? who's to say? i'd like a friend to take me out to dinner, first at provence, then at chez nous (chestnut) & later at i don't know where but nobody does that here, it's surprising we have enough to eat given the stinkpotnesses of trump but now our food is covered by chemicals & in an imminent nuclear war we'll be annihilated anyway, in this world, on this globe, people not only have not enough to eat but very few doctors for tons of them meanwhile one of the princes of england is being touted for marrying a mixed-race dame because the royal family couldn't react otherwise & the people who voted for trump don't seem to care if he doesn't do what he says, they just like him(?)—how could that be?

there's an explosion of women accusing men of sexual harassment, I'm sure every single woman who's left her house has experienced this, not always with famous men, just men with testosterone, ask any sex-change female, it's a tricky situation, you really can't be a man, a real man, you'd better go to camp; women have just put up with it because people told them they have to, but they don't, men can control themselves, they don't have to beat anybody up, all those gory t.v. shows, all the blood, the blood spattered or splattered on the faces of others, even in africa, people get murdered or their legs blown off & then there's slavery as recently as now, hunting, violence, it's all got to go, sorry, you were right, you won't be able to defend yourself when the govt. tries to take over so don't bother to grow big & tall, hefty like a gorilla, they're on their way out too but not for the same reasons, everything's the fault of the stupid humans as if they didn't have the brains developed to let the world be as it will be with all the complex fractals & designs to inspire us to all be kinds of sunflowers, we blew it. i see blue because someone in my species blew it. testosterone has a lot of 'e's in it. but 'w's aren't blue but they can be for now, or for new. a new blue 'e' might stand for anything on door or deer. the blue lights reflect on the trees which are now blue too. used to be blue xmas lights emanated from a jewish house, now subsumed by xians too, now reflecting on xian forests too ALL THAT GREEN PAPER!

once upon a time, every vowel was an 'e,' so there! thes wes et the begenneng of teme & nebedy noticed et yet. en fect et wes fen. when peeple ferfet te heve fen they mede these ether vewels, so whet the feck? e dent de et. we ceedl've getten by weth jest 'e's ceedn't we? The roblem wes the 'e's were blut net green, i felt. er were they green net blee? whech wes et? well we ever knew? who ceres? e'm cenfesed by the blee leghts. they weren't lettle. theegh. & E wes green. e dednt de et. bet whe ded et? whe mede the letters celers fer ell the synesthetes en the world? we blend eer senses tegether en eer bebyheed & seme remeens, semte-mes ets celers letteres, sometimes shepes & seends, ether temes ether steff. ef yee hed e gerl, yee'd meke the nersery penk. maybe. e dent knew. E es green, net blee. thes es my fenel enswer. ferever green er blee. which es et? cen yee tell? ef e tern the blee leghts en, well e see the blee leghts en elways? e'm sere semebedy's dene thes beferes

"it's queer, i seem to remember my future works, although i don't even know what they will be about." nabokov, "the gift."

there's no way to say with enough venom that in the relatively brief time he's pretended to be the president, trump has done more damage to the environment, to immigrants, to income equality, to education, to health than anyone can ever conceive. there are lawsuits in the works but they might not do it; everything sounds not vehement enough—will there soon be a law against clouds in the sky? ellsberg who was a nuclear war planner(!) before whistle-blower talks on amy goodman about how many people'd be killed in a nuclear war. answer: all. nothing edible. we grew up thinking there'd be a nuclear war; now again, time to eat up all the cheddar cheese rabbits, they're organic. the atlas of *the world's staring at us. read? why? will there always be this threat or is it just at the start & end of life? is it imaginary? dream? you can hear the coyote but not see it. opposite of children. coltsfoot, locust tree. bye.*

who else would have a memory of the future, it's all i can think about. i'm guessing blake did & psychics of course, hannah never talked about it, of what use is it? i found this memory of the future in the garbage can, in that place, in the dump. leftover popovers. pike quenelles. i have an itch.

I IMAGINE A POEM by bernadette mayer
(based on the poem by ALAN CASLINE)

Some extraordinary things have happened. once
in red rock (Red Rock) near here i did see a rainbow in
the middle of the woods & the sun wasn't even out. instead
of thinking it was magic, i thought that's unusual
but red rock is a very unusual place, partly because
so many animals were there. the first time we drove up
to the house, there was a luna moth on the screen, like
an emblem. (even now the vacuum cleaner sounds like
it's rehearsing a poem.) red rock was a good place to
walk because all the roads were dirt. once, while
walking a car came up behind me & bumped me as if
encouraging me to go faster, the way they bump cars
in canada. once i went out into a dense fog & could hear
a deer snorting next to me. before that, in great barrington
a flying squirrel moved into my house. i'd put tomatoes
in strategic spots so it'd have to glide to them; it slept
in the kitchen drawer. in some house, i think it was
the one in lake buel, there were mushrooms coming up in
the shower. i dare you to make this a real poem, half
as wide & with all the sounds of the angelic choirs
of poetry, or, of the homelessness of poetry, or the wild
thyme-ish-ness of poetry. i wouldn't say this of many
words but the word poetry would be stupid if it didn't have
such a good etymology. like engineer. once on the appalachian
trail, birds came around phil's head. now there is a
hiatus for xmas, but why? marie, sophie, lewis, kat,
brenda & atticus are coming for some meal, oh & don & akram.
i have no myrrh so it'll be quail eggs. what's the top
of the mountain to me, has a tree so if you went up there
you could use it for xmas, decorated with electric blue
bulbs or candles and seahorses, i'd like a multi-colored
seahorse candle.

it's the eve of solstice, eve of the solstice. light! hurry! every time we turn the blue lights on they reflect on the trees in the field. you could have a xmas tree that's just a reflection. i am not at all sorry for my sins—so there! what a dumb time of year for people who don't have families. trump's decided to stop giving money to starving people. the blue trees glisten too. the blue lights shine on the black car, on the brown trees, on the chickadees. i had a red blood test— in winter it rains. blue climbs the tree like blooms. blues climb the trees like blooms.

it didn't snow yet. i don't know snow, i wouldn't know snow if it pinched my ass, if snow pinched my ass. i'd like an ass-pinch of snow, every ass is different. put your ass in the dryer, to stay up late i learn about aerial ireland, the queen at 90, burma, the mayans in georgia & the copper dilemma, all those mounds, magic, the lengthening of the head like extraterrestrials but how did the may-ans get to georgia, did they build the mounds in alabama too. it's so gloomy, there was a fire up the road, right by the fire chief's house, colors you can't see

make room for colors you can never see, wait, colors you can't see—can you never see them? it's called the visible spectrum, my money's on the invisible spectrum, just cause you can't see it don't mean you could never see it. think of the jot! for instance why do people mix together time & space? a chipmunk wouldn't.

it seems like everybody fights & kills. across the road bill has 5 shotguns.

i'd still like to live in a cave, maybe the denisova cave & i wish nobody i ever knew was dead, much less almost everybody and when i get to the end of this page, it'll all be over

now the snowing, whiteouting & blowing but bill & phil talked to each other standing. it was a fine mist of a snow but now big blusters blow from the porch roof & i can't find any books to read. i'm trying rhino ranch. rebecca solnit's save dreams worked 4 a while as did alexander kluge, soon it'll have to be duane's depressed! oh no not again! sad is it around here, no indoor pools, no sunlight. i know the days are getting longer, how could they not? the shortest one's passed. kluge notes that rudolf steiner asks what chance sense means. in *this case taking two little girls off a plane that crashed. i've been at the end of my tether before*

i wish i lived in the path between heaps of lapis lazuli stones in afghanistan which is the only place they are, lithium in chile & colorado, rare earth in i don't know but used to, a monster crawled across the top of the hill where the evergreen tree is, it must've been three times the size of a mountain lion, darling, let's give it a sugar cookie 3x the size of itself, i'm so sad, i'm the color of sad snow. it's freezing cold, half the creek is frozen, it's freezing in here too, i mean i'm freezing because of being old, should spend old age in sauna, sweat lodge, south, desert, oven, fire, on game of thrones all the zombies fell into the frozen water plus the dragon which perhaps will be resuscitated as a zombie dragon to fight the survivors of the 7 kingdoms under the ice, well well i'll see you soon it's not even the end of this year

the back porch is sinking because of the rain, the birdbath is overflowing, the squirrels are freaking out, you'd better hurry up, the world might be over soon, the geese have taken to the trees, or crows, easily. i ate a cherry-plum, the hybrid age, who is the 'I'? the I is a why, a festival nest of Death, if Death is an eye and rain fell on it, living in the united states—which are really not united at all, what a farce—you can hear, as almost anywhere, the sounds from the birds nest festival behind your head outside the house on a ledge painted yellow as if the birds were finches, well maybe they are, who would ever know if they weren't? or who would know if they were? well that's a question, but who would ever know if it's a question?

my house is crooked, i stole your song before you sang it, the icicles've stopped dripping, first it snowed, then it got sunny, now it's all cloudy like some enchanted evening, a yacht is useless when it's in the cold cold repair shop.

gloomy today, it's the gloomiest. in the ocean shellfish don't have enough calcium carbonate to make their shells, as in acid rain. "anthropocene" might be the end of the world, literally. however that's said it's all wrong. for one thing it'd be kind of hard to end the world via pollution. starvation, maybe, no growing season, probably, a violent cataclysm, maybe all the dinosaurs will come back & gobble up all the humans—what a place to be left, east nassau

69

overrun with deer ticks, but who will they eat? just one human? giant deer
ticks could a good horror movie make. begonias from last year still left pink on
the stems, connected to the stems so maybe this is a sign that in nature things
don't do what you'd think they do. a greenhouse, a hotbed, glowing fluores-
cent, petrified, implicated, political wood, wooden as a politician, simplified
as an inflorescence, creatures go to great lengths for their potential mates, like
incipient periwinkles, dark pink begonias, ever-darkening skies, the sight of
the color of the sky, when it's blue. will the world end before the cables are put
underground? will putting the cables underground end at the world? apropos
of not this, phil suggested i have two address books, one i can find & one i can't
find.

i have no doubt, as long as i live, that i will go to museums, eyeing the dapper
& misused paintings as if it was my supper, served on a placemat with a knife,
fork & spoon & for dessert there will be that gelatinized cream called pina co-
lada, no, i mean pinto beans, no, i mean i never forget the word clafouti, then
why cook as i didn't do, i don't think anybody even likes this i can't remem-
ber, try. it's jiggling like jello & it begins with a 'p,' maybe, pinstripe potatoes,
passepartout, it's only four yet it seems way past, past the paste? heavy cream
we seem to have but quotidian fun does not dwell here, oh here comes panna
cotta, it's like panna grady, she was a rich one, so coated with clotted cream,
wood to burn, a wooden man, will he gelatinize?

utopia + letter-color broadside
hologram? typewriter in hotel
backdrop of drawings of everything by youkumamoto oysters political?
assad! rohingya, etc.

slight night overburdened with coxcombs it will not be spring yet tomorrow &
you won't see the red blue moon ever again because time has hidden the cold, it
will sneak out from under the bed like coming or going might when the inch-
worm's head glows & creates a clone, of course it's female

here it is gloomy again & cold-ish, the maple syrup–making seems to be
continuing but now with the sugar shack looming boiling is most likely to be
being done, we're guessing. a lot of hay is going by. so there we stopped at

max, alyssa & zola's house to catch a cold. in my old age i should be living in
a bubble. i developed pneumonia and, after studying the space which is huge
but cannot hold much weight (no wrecking ball), wound up in a hospital, my
head full of the arguments between nabokov & edmund wilson whose dressing
room for their public arguments was right next to my hospital bed, to which
i was constantly being told to get back (in). there was a feeling of freedom for
a moment then, sort of, here, there've been 2 now famous nor'easters, a lot of
snow but the third one's gone out to sea. maybe. escaped from the hosp. place
& journeyed somehow & uglily, back onto the plane, to newark, a hideous
motel full of heavy carrot cake, to harlem to get the car, forgot cold waiting
room, then to here, no greeting of course, but this house is livable in & luckily
we remembered we live here. the begonias are thriving, a darker pink than i'd
remembered

Pinwheels are innocent
New days not befouled by S
Ense, new handkerchiefs
Under old handkerchiefs
Mist under a tree or two hovering
Over where the sun sets
Never looking like it
Insouciant as an ingenue or
An apricot ricocheting, then boomeranging
well the sky is gray, so gray, it couldn't be grayer,
it's as gray as a loophole.

there's a butterfly on this machine, there's a butterfly on every machine, is it
to be beautiful that we aim, not now, no not now nonenervatingly gustato-
rily, which food was in which book, wilhelm asked, or did he? i wonder why
we always they always they me you see become lacking in self esteem when
nobody's looking, i mean and women when somebody is, i wonder why it
seems like in the ugly mirror i see two bedposts & a lamp, leaning i can see
three, there are three corners over the extra one in the corner, i think it was the
coffee bean says, in french, may we pour you a cup? a cup of what? absinthe?
casually like an opportunity, nobody out to get me, are thee? my horror is an
honor & i am not satisfied by my stay therefore i am dusting, little do i know

it but the upper corners of the visible rectangles are thoroughly ingratiatingly
covered with stinkbugs while beneath them is are was were wherein i have
found it to be the lair of spiderlikethings, a kind of spidery commons, but it's
the deer ticks that make our lives corruptible & while they ride over the river &
through the woods, they do not go to grandmother's house at all in their little
scarlet tanager coats & caps, they are on their way to a bed upstairs ominously
& stupendously like in jail but you're innocent, will it ever be the time of the
scorpions, whenever i think of scorpions in books i mean boots, i think of you,
oh, steel and aluminum i didn't sleep again but i must have slept under those
resounding sheets somewhere you'll find the sleep-residue glowing yellow,
getting revenge in guatemala, my biological dad has changed the land, upsy
daisy, turned over the flood & we will be enthroned on A MOUNTAIN TOP
WHERE THERE'S itsy bitsy spiders willing & able to wear white clothes
over and over, only white like meals, no color in them, boy was it blowsy and
weepy, nevertheless punishing russia, willow tit willow wonderbar marienbad
over there last year at marienbad we went home: stein, hawthorne, kerouac
& maybe more for a class. put clark in there. shakespeare.. i, BM, am toler-
ating some weepiness & meeting a guy who seemed to know s-thing about
syria, notes are often never read again, you never knew what you meant, the
peregrine falcon. twice we went to the pod, the weird pod lobster & duck fried
rice & something lo mein (hotter) THE INN AT PENN, TOODLE-OO
and, no, a shortened form of psychoanalysis, dead as a doorknob, eh? or, neh?
soon soon, the begonias are still with us, the sky is gray, the rain it's raining on
robert walser and on the ships at sea, most snow has melted, the flood insur-
ance isn't a realistic thing: still grayness crossed by still black wire, there is no
beauty in it. whole, partial, minuscule, dot. should i or not? is it real with the
horse not in it? that light's too close to the woodstove. are words but designs
when looked over as if they were a gray sky? did you do it? black, but really
brown, tree limbs against the silly sky that doesn't fall, no clouds—will there be
a storm?

this ribbon might be the one, it might be the sun
a sharpened pencil, a necklace, a sitting santa claus
the bears are coming; the birds aren't here
clouds in the sky

if a bear, get to see a bear, destroy a bird
feeder—it's easter, it's not easter, april fool's
a crack in the glass, glass beads, how tall is the bear,
reusable stickers fell down, the spanish book fell down,
why did "they" send me it? there might be chives
although i am female, i still root for investigative poetry
like making maple syrup; though there are no buds on the
trees yet, i have written a history of troy, ny in poetry & it's
just a beginning
though the field is empty, a few leaves
are blessing sometimes like ice cubes made of leftover wine
there's a crack in this window
it's no hurricane the leaves are flying before
would an ice cube blow slower than a leaf
would a bullet meant for a bison in a hurricane go faster than
an ice cube? there's a chickadee
a word from homeric hymn is: greatest
the squirrel baffler is moving faster than the bird balancer

across the field are the little leaves, oregano oil, wild columbines, bar-
tholomew's cobble. all play, play all, behind the barren trees are leaves, behind
the barren trees are the leaves of other trees, bushes beginning, bush leagues,
bush leaves, leagues of leaves, a league of leaves, heavy leaves, heavenly
leaf-blowing leagues, major leagues of leaves, the leaves' minor leagues, saw
hundreds of millions of trout lilies in bloom in the PSF + the hepatica & maybe
some yellow violets! can't find MILKWEED SMITHEREENS ANY-
WHERE. WHERE COULD IT HAVE GOTTEN TO?
new spring green leaves on almost everything

Sonnet Bill DeNoyelles

Is the work in loud waiting color secrets to be done
Like if we mention the overlooked haunted house displays
Counting both the hiking & the hitchhiking rainbow families
Dear mother dear mother the church is cold the church
Is cold is only a form of William Blake's daily life's
Permitting the sights of concepts' prearranged numberings

I will show you rectangles, there were the mountain laurels
Of the houses & the people to their not drawn breath lines
Transforming a meadow to what they call straight lines
The baptized enclave of the non-saintly sun set & rise
By holding the thought of love absolutized in July
There were faces & arms when no figures appeared, he

At noon shows a view: It's what we see out the window
Yet I know it's a picture of the house from which we look, in which we all live.

finches having fun, white violets going it alone,
making tzatziki
things coming up in the house: nasturtiums, canna lilies
savory memory

should i have a cube?
i have been waiting so long for you to pay me,
i wonder if it's just that i am so unpayable
because i am a female. there's been a lot of talk
about this lately, people even losing their jobs
because they haven't paid females, I wonder ... forced
poverty? is it the same as sex?
saw a real butterfly
today, not just the white ones. there will be so many lilacs, it looks like.
it looks like lilacs & violets & late buds. the sun is going away,
phil is chainsawing,
how much do i know now that i'm so ancient?
i don't feel very knowledgeable at all, a cardinal at the feeder! with a purple
finch. white
violets, did i already say that? blooming alone
in a clump.
all the finches are purple today.

i'm 73 now it's the 14th of may, it's only violet & dandelion time, i will empty
the dishwasher, make lunch, then make a snack for phil, no orioles yet. rocks,
flowers, birds, trees. mushrooms, atmosphere, ghosts, supernatural things,
would that be ghosts? otherworldly things, it's a wordy yet worldly world or
word but why do i live in it? early spring yet may retarded by a batch of cold
even snowy weather, radishes? the sun makes color charts fade, the humming-
bird never came, there's a hummingbird! it's gray like preparing for the rain.
the front may be moving in, it's getting humider & humider, i'm sweating in
my i'm nobody shirt, marie sent me two apricot-related presents so far, there's
one more. deborah sounds a bit nuts, viz. my naturopath. helen's not only come
over to ask me a few nosy taken me under questions ending in "it's not easy
getting old, is it" but came back to tell me we're under a tornado watch & now
it's the calm before the storm, sorry, storm & helen, i'll read my book or drink

wine, 2 hummingbirds thunder, crack, big dark cloud like a hairpiece spring
green against the dark sky like for a rainbow, so many 'k's, a whoosh, thun-
der-clap-like, the lilacs are seeming ready, a little lightning, saw bolt, saw bolt
again, heard crack, now no tornado, over there, all i see is robins
the sun's up, not out, i am subject to paranoid fantasies
i just saw a groundhog, it was real though.
i peeled potatoes but peeling a really small potato, when there are limitless
amounts of them, is frustrating, peeling huge potatoes is better, these potatoes
have a lot of eyes & weird things, one was totally out of the question then the
chipmunk came in the house so we came in & he or she went out again or in
again so it could do the other, the chipmunk doesn't owe me any money that
i know of & no kind of pleasure is taken in anything no matter how many of
those things there are & what color too though some pleasure might be taken in
a new color, one we've never seen before, i will come to thee, never will i, i lost
my shoes in one of the many rooms, the stanzas of the dream, it was near a door
i tried to slip through without losing my shoes but i lost i mean i lost my shoes,
the opening was too small, it pushed my shoes off, i remembered it very well,
even though it was just a dream, why do people say that, "just"? things to do:

> *pay me poem*
> *syria poem*
> *eat lunch*

i agree to find the holy grail if you pay me a poem, i agree to go to syria if you
write me a poem, i agree to eat, i mean to write you a poem about lunch if
you'll tell me everything about syria, i agree to pay for lunch in syria if you'll,
i don't know. it'd be expensive to have lunch in syria but maybe we'd learn
something.

there's a stuffed bee on a broken typewriter. the sky is white; there are white
violets. hardly anybody walks in the woods or thru the high
grass or lies down in it where you might see an indian
pipe or the roots of one—are there roots? it's time
for ice cream, maybe next time it rains, it'll rain
ice cream, why you care if you get lyme disease is if you have
it long enough is affects your brain & exacerbates arthritis
i dreamt that i lost my shoes by going thru a narrow

space that pulled them off
memories of the poetry state
forest, or, one field guide a week.

it's thursday & i have no power to come & go near grass, tree branches or nests
of deer ticks. we are not alone but we are alone. those times there was that
fear were practice or showing you that when you're alone, you don't have to be
scared. but perhaps you do. having a philosophy or a god might help but then
think of all the problems that would cause. gods & philosophies inevitably let
you down. once i had a boyfriend who told me that as long as i was with him,
nothing would happen to me. the poison plants are growing a deeper purple.
though we've all gotten used to killing, that is, the putting an end to an al-
ready-existing human life, it violates the laws of equilibrium & what to do with
the remains? the best idea i've heard is to sew the body in a shroud made with
mushroom spores & bury it like a bulb or corn. short of that i'd like to create
a space the size of me, then get somebody to shoot me dead & cover me over.
before that i could cover myself with seeds or even a mat of heirloom tomatoes.
or heirloom weeds.

i'm reading nabokov's "insomniac dreams" which is an attempt to prove this
guy dunne's theory that dreams are precognitive. written by n's translator
gennady bar-something including n's dream journal which is also his wife
vera's. i see a fly & a stinkbug. creme brulee was the answer to today's jumble.
2 stinkbugs—where do they go at night? under the daybed? the stinkbug's right
there like a miniature prehistoric dinosaur except with antennae, staring at
me; i can smell the cedar oil tick repellent ... i work here (back porch) when
the sun's out & in there when it's not, it's cold in the not-room & not in the is-
room, i think many of us know that dreams can be precognitive but we couldn't
"prove" it, the concept of prove is kind of stupid, but whales know they are, so
we've learned from them but not everyone would learn from a whale i guess
& i couldn't prove that from a whale's perspective everything is precognitive
including lampshades

Untitled Poem

from now on there will be no fun
nobody can even snicker much less
laugh out loud, secret underground tapes
tapes of laughter will circulate & if

you get caught with a laughter tape
you will pay more than if you had sex
laughing during sex results in siberian
trees falling on your house & plus

you must live with trump forever in a casino
to create a nuclear summer-fall-winter-spring's
no laughing matter, you'll have nothing to eat
nothing will grow that's edible

crop-sprayers like demons will render all
your vegetables poison & you will become
a republican determined to destroy the joy
of all & you will become a republican

of the sort that creates explosions
showering gold on corporations like a kilonova
while the other classes can't even eat fruit
you think instead of peas you can eat pears

but even the tomatoes will be wasted like
helicopters looking in vain for marijuana
& don't go to madagascar; they're having the plague
dig your caves now & laugh in them pronto

car whack symptom of sardines weather our friends
& acquaintances at funerals in tenements it's
scintillating to fight & die for our car culture
with its breathtaking gas stations & brutalist

architecture of howard mcdonalds &
sex isn't illegal as long as you abuse the female
but let's get to the meat of it: this guy
has got to go, chance & pence & thence

they're both so dense & frumpy, hence
i think how long will i have to spend on death row
or will i die before they kill me
in a mall, school or church shooting

or maybe i'll go even crazier
& they'll let me get a gun
so i can shoot you & then me
& together we'll go to the abyss of doom

a fancy hotel in either heaven or hell
at $5,000 a night featuring fake squid
rolled in RARE ARTIFICIAL FLAVORS, handcrafted
raspberries dribbled over fresh ticks

with music by a transgender trump look-alike
& a group of black break-dancers
performing their greatest hits FUCK WHITE SUPREMACY
& WHOSE SIDE ARE YOU ON? until the dressing gong rings

Carnival

It was a sunny cold day when
yellow petals of tulips fell
on our table here and there

when science setups said so
because who knows which scene
is not to be forgotten
like chocolate flowers in view

this is a very letter-*s* obsessed science
setup, such a splendid yellow scene

even the chocolate tulip is yellow
in as much as it's sleep, naps are yellow
as in super bowl, snowy owl

suppertime owl hoot heard in the night
we stop chewing in disbelief
no candles lit, no coffee on the stove
on the other side of a closed window
we hear

the owl was letting us know
not to forget about it
an all-sex owl on the tree-of-life porch maybe

poetry porch life for all
leave your troubles at the door
bring fresh baked goods and more
we will play the waiting game and
guess the color of the next tractor

for brown and white eggs we have
an ancient scissor
with a rooster as a clue
to lop off the top of each soft-boiled
before you dip the sticks of toast
into the center

WITH PHILIP GOOD, FEBRUARY 2022

it's friday july 13th, the fat squirrel's tail's gotten longer, why? cause i say so! &
listen up here to my tale of a tail, it's not a tell-tale either but rather a tee-
ny-weeny tale on the nightly news. & that includes you too Dr. Death circling
around like a hippopotamus or marsupial in my yard, who's in charge? do
i care? holy, holy, intervademecum. so what if i die? will the hepatica? the
hepatica will never die, like a person, reliably always there though just a mile
over, but will the indian pipe ever reappear? i will never know, or, i may never
know, now, some rumbling, light flashing darkness o'er the land, rain! no
porches fell down, this ear is crumbling, (thunder speaking), hiding chip-
munks, flying crows, coverlet curlicues, a bouncing petunia, a rain-drummed
petunia, crow near the snapped-off tree

my chair got rained on
more than it got sat in

Early Spring?

can't find "mind of hour," the sun's coming out
three men stand talking at the field edge
you see, maple syrup season's already here
maybe, at least they put the buckets up
on the trees, that is, like the delights
of roaming after, like the tree that defended
the forest, it's only February, repeated
early springs exacerbate doubt & droughts,
if you will, plus the finches are here, how
could that be? birds can't be wrong, meaning
is not a message or physiognomy, there was a
crescent moon right by Venus in the sky to tell us
to try Poe for once, an early spring might be
the backyard is covered with moss but in the end
it will be sooner that everybody's snowmobile
is for sale, they can't still be talking there
on the field edge, Bill sitting in my chair
representing calm in chaos, Phil standing seeming
to be reason & Jay shouting because he's hard
of hearing, the whole local gang's there, I saw
somebody walk by as if the war's over my friend

Bear in Mind

bear in window
bears in mind

bears in the wind
bear in winter

bare in mind
beer in mind

bear in mind
bearing minds

mindless bear
barring minds

bear in mind
bear in midwinter

bear in mind
bear on your mind

hear in mind
hear in the wind

read your mind
bear in mind

read and mind
bearing in mind

Conclusion

The Method of Repeated Reproduction of
remembered material with increasing lapse
of time, until it has reached a stereotyped
form through transformations in which influences
play, excites an attitude of uncertainty, which
has nothing to do with objective inaccuracy,
towards the introduction of what is new.